This Was On My Mind

MY Daily Meditations Shared In Book Form

(Note: Space For Your Comments/Meditations And Journaling Are Included)

LORIE HALE

WESTBOW
P R E S S®
A DIVISION OF THOMAS NELSON
& ZONDERVAN

WestBow Press books may be ordered through booksellers or by contacting:

WestBow Press
A Division of Thomas Nelson & Zondervan
1663 Liberty Drive
Bloomington, IN 47403
www.westbowpress.com
844-714-3454

Scripture taken from the King James Version of the Bible.

ISBN: 978-1-6642-5668-2 (sc)
ISBN: 978-1-6642-5667-5 (e)

Print information available on the last page.

WestBow Press rev. date: 1/31/2022

FOREWORD

BY

Hugh A Hale

I am glad and excited to be a part of this book. I am Godly Proud of my wife and "Sweet Tulip" Lorie. I have always told her that she has wisdom beyond her years. This comes to her as a result of her sincerity toward GOD and her humble spirit. She is a praying woman and has a genuine love for GOD and His word. This will be clear and evident as you read and glean from the Rich Golden Nuggets of Wisdom in this book. I have also told her on more than one occasion that she was excellent in journaling and note taking. I encourage everyone to take advantage of the enrichment of this read. This Daily Devotional will Help Give Guidance, Courage and Strength in our Work with The LORD.

- Hugh Hale, Pastor-

Powerful New Life Church

1300 Riverside Avenue, Kingsport, TN, 37660

DEDICATED TO

All Deep Christian Thinkers Such as My Husband Elder Hugh Hale

THANK YOU!

For sometime now, I've worked on 3-4 books at one time! I decided Finally that I would finish one! Some of these thoughts I have shared in conversation but Much of them I haven't, so I thought rather, I'd write a book! In writing a book, people can Choose to read at his/her own risk or Pleasure, whatever it may be to the Reader!

Enjoy... I Pray

ACKNOWLEDGEMENTS

I'd like to express my gratitude to GOD number one, for being my All in All, my Everything and I could go on and on! Also, for my husband/Pastor Hugh Hale who supports me in every endeavor and who has told me that he thinks I can do anything, and of course, Only through GOD! Thank you Powerful New Life Church for all the love and support given down through the years! To my late Dad (May, 1940- May 5, 2021) who had a big part in my existence and whom I believe is in The Presence of GOD this very moment! Last but not least, my Mother (Sarah Ford) who has been a Constant in my life!!! Love you Mama! You're the Strongest person I know!

CONTENTS

CHAPTER 1

Be Strong

Philippians 4:13
"I can do all things through CHRIST which strengtheneth me".
Joel 3:10 (partial)
"........let the weak say, I am strong".(KJV)

If the strong are weak, what shall the True weak do?!

The LORD allowed this thought to come to mind several years ago. It's thought provoking! In other words, if those who know how to live Holy, become weak .... what example will those who follow, have?!

YOUR THOUGHTS:

CHAPTER 2

Listen

We have to Really keep our ears close to GODS mouth in these last days! We need to Make sure we know His voice so we Don't heed that of a stranger! Ask Him to order your steps daily and if He says Don't Go That Way ... Then don't go! Be wise and not too mouthy, I'm learning! Be Humble like CHRIST our example! He never bragged on Himself.... they asked and He spoke Truth!

Ex: "Then said they all, Art thou then the Son of God? And he said unto them, Ye say that I am". Luke 22:70 (KJV)

Proverbs 18:16 Says, "A man's gift makes room for him, and bringeth him before great men". (KJV) And again Proverbs 27:2. "Let another man praise thee, and not thine own mouth; a stranger, and not thine own lips". (KJV)

Sometimes it may be necessary to give your resume but only when Necessary! Apostle Paul did it often and we should understand why... he persecuted the Church but later became a follower then Leader! Paul wanted other Believers and Unbelievers to Know that he had been changed through The Power of CHRIST! We must check our motives and Then proceed with our resume!

YOUR THOUGHTS:

CHAPTER 3

Stay

One Thing I'm Learning In My Christian Walk is to ....Just Stay! When Misunderstood, Talked About, Judged By Flesh, Mocked, Ridiculed, Walked On, Belittled, Lied On and To,..... ENDURE! Only GOD Can Do It Through You! It's Easy to quit or leave but it takes a firm grip on Faith to Stay! Power To Stay! Holy Ghost Power! You will Not regret Staying when it is in the plan of GOD!

*Read: Ephesians 6:13-17 ((KJV)

YOUR THOUGHTS:

CHAPTER 4

Don't Expect Godliness From The World

12/19/2018

When one expects too much from The world, (example: I don't want to expect people to treat me with kindness Just Because I treat them with kindness) emotions get involved and discrimination and hurt feelings are present! GOD created Humanity to be Beautiful, but when one group feel they are on a higher intellectual level, more intelligent, a higher Class (due to Name, Money or Other Status Quo including Culture) than Another Group.....That's a Real Problem! I'm learning not to expect Too much so that I'm not provoked to be rude As well!! Read Matthew 7:12

YOUR THOUGHTS:

CHAPTER 5

This Thing Is Serious

Jan. 1,2019

Man! Being a Leader In or over Anything is So SERIOUS! Rules are made to keep Order, but If when rules are broken and there are no consequences...It is a Real Problem! However, if that/ those particular Leader/s aren't following the Rules themselves... that's a Worse problem because they're not being examples! Now, Mercy is a New Ballgame! GOD shows mercy through people toward others and that's what Believers call Blessings and Answered prayer! 1 Thessalonians 5:14 (KJV) is a good read!

YOUR THOUGHTS:

CHAPTER 6

Check It Off

Jan 6,2019

Does This Speak To You?!

There are some things I Just Don't Want To Do! However, in those times, I Do It Anyway! I Do It Through GOD By Faith and Even Scared Sometimes but the fear disappears Once I move Forward. I say, "LORD help me to get through This", and check it off my list of Difficulties! And Then.... Next, Next, Next, I am a gazing stock, but it's for GODS Glory! (Paraphrased)

Read Hebrews 10:33 (KJV)

YOUR THOUGHTS:

CHAPTER 7

No Fear

2 Timothy 1:7 (KJV)

"For GOD hath not given me the spirit of fear; but of
power, and of love, and of a sound mind".

I will remain calm and give it to GOD! I refuse to allow the Noise that This Storm makes,
cause me to become Nervous or Anxious or Fearful!

YOUR THOUGHTS:

CHAPTER 8

Discernment

Discernment is a Powerful gift from GODS Spirit! We are shown things so we can pray earnestly concerning them, in hopes that issues are resolved and deliverance will take place! However, if a thing/s are not dealt with Properly, in a timely manner.... it then becomes a problem that can't be handled low key! (Read proverbs 27:5) (KJV)

YOUR THOUGHTS:

CHAPTER 9

Can You Handle The TRUTH

Some say, just tell me the Truth, I won't get mad! The Truth is, some of Us can't handle it! I've been guilty of Not being able to handle the Truth at Times Too, but I'm Learning that the Truth makes us Free! Mature persons have learned to handle the truth because it's necessary! Read John 8:32 (KJV)

YOUR THOUGHTS:

CHAPTER 10

Maturity Check

2/13/2019

We can't afford to be immature! It's past time to Grow Up! Some of us have been saved 10, 20, 30 years or More! LORD help us to be the Mature Believers we say that we are! I'm learning to simply Get Over It! Whatever IT is! I want to see JESUS in peace! If my feelings get hurt... So What! Get Over It (even though it may take time), keep moving forward in the faith process! I have Not Arrived but I'm Learning! Accept what GOD allows because obviously, whatever it is, received permission from The LORD first! Think about that! Read Ephesians 4:13-16 (KJV)

YOUR THOUGHTS:

CHAPTER 11

Who Are You Asking

Don't go to sheep for shepherd business. How can they understand?

Read Titus 2 (The whole chapter). (KJV)

YOUR THOUGHTS:

CHAPTER 12

Valiant and Virtuous

2/19/19

So I learned that the word Virtuous (for a woman) has a similar meaning as Valiant (for a man) in scripture! Valiant means- brave, fearless, courageous, unalarmed, heroic and lion hearted (to name a few descriptions). Virtuous- showing or having High moral standards, clean, righteous (few descriptions). For example: Proverbs 31:10 Who can find a Virtuous woman? For her price is far above rubies! (KJV) They're hard to find! They can't be found easily because they're hid in GOD! One must go through The Blood of JESUS to find her! Their price is High because she's rare! The same goes for a Valiant man! A Virtuous woman is not moved (necessarily) by what a man possesses, but rather who possesses the man! Meaning GOD! Godly men, seek a Virtuous woman... one who serves GOD and because of That, won't forsake you! One who ain't scared (excuse my English)! (Trying to keep it Brief but I could go on))!

YOUR THOUGHTS:

CHAPTER 13

Can You See

2-22-19

Put Your Blinders On! Not so you can't see CHRIST, but Rather so you can't see man (Flesh)! It might be a good idea to distribute the darkest of shades (sun glasses) at the church entrance? Sight is a Great gift... don't get me wrong... however, we mustn't defeat the purpose of assembling together as Believers in The Church House! Too many are star struck, and that would be Great if we were looking at The Star, which is CHRIST! Well even CHRIST (and He's LORD) said not to call Him good because Only GOD is Good! What About Us?! It Really takes Something in these Last days to stay Humble because we live in Such a Self/Star struck society, But We Must!!!!! Only Through The SPIRIT of GOD is this Possible!!! HE keeps Everything in perspective! What we must know is that, when scripture speaks of falling away, it doesn't Necessarily just mean, out of the church building or away from the church world (so to speak) but Mainly out of Fellowship with CHRIST Himself!!! Relationship is Key! What will Really Help us to stay close and therefore Humble is spending Quality/Necessary Time In GODS Presence! It's tough to do at Times but in order to stay in Order with The Word, we just have to make time!

Let's be determined, that when we arrive at the House we gather to Worship that we go with our Full/ Whole attention and focus on The Star Himself and Not on the containers that He Indwells! LORD I want to be a True Worshipper! I need You LORD A good read is Hebrews 12:2. (KJV)

YOUR THOUGHTS:

CHAPTER 14

GOD Answers

3-5-19

John 11:30-37 (KJV)

Behold, how He loved him! (John 11:36 partial)

It's not that JESUS isn't concerned about our daily woes that come to His followers.... but He knows the end result! He knows that He has Already given us the Victory Regardless!

In verse 37, JESUS answered a question about could He have prevented Lazarus' death? And the answer,... Of course He could, And these are the same questions unbelievers are asking today! We need to study up on The Word of GOD so that He can bring it back to our remembrance, when necessary! (Partial- (KJV)) 2 Timothy 2:15.

YOUR THOUGHTS:

CHAPTER 15

Wait For Good

3/15/19

Some will take as much time as needed to fulfill an evil plan, as did Absalom when he murdered his brother Amnon for raping his half Sister! (Which was Horrible)! However, to wait to do evil was Wrong as well! He waited 2 years!

Joseph waited 13 years before the promised prophecy was fulfilled! Don't wait to do evil but wait for The Promise!!! Wait for the good!

A good read! Psalm 27:14. (KJV)

Note: Read more on King David and his Son Absalom beginning in 2 Samuel 13! (KJV).

YOUR THOUGHTS:

CHAPTER 16

Just STOP It

4-12-19

The blind Can't lead the blind! Please STOP going to Weak people for Spiritual advice!

Read Luke 6:39

YOUR THOUGHTS:

CHAPTER 17

Can You Tell Time

4-26-2019

Wanting to be immature, But knowing that immaturity has played out! As the older Saints/ Believers would say, the sun is almost down .... the day is almost over! What they were saying was this, JESUS is soon to come and we'd all better get our act together! John 9:4 (KJV) Says it best, "I must work the works of him that sent me, while it is day: the night cometh, when no man can work."

YOUR THOUGHTS:

CHAPTER 18

Be Quiet/ You'll Thank GOD Later

6-4-2019

Sometimes it's Best to let people sit in quietness.... Often, if they open their mouths at that particular time, you may not want to hear what comes from their heart! Let them think on it and talk to GOD about it First!!!

I'm personally, Learning to keep silent before saying something I'll regret later! Even if I am, or appear to be moody... trust me, it's better I do that than hurt feelings Through The Process!!!

The Silent treatment is Better than Angry Noise!

A good read! Acts 19:36 (KJV)

YOUR THOUGHTS:

CHAPTER 19

You Can Handle It

6-5-2019

You may Think you can't handle It Anymore, (whatever your It May be), but just give GOD time to work on you! By then (when the time comes) You Can!!! Read Philippians 4:13 (KJV)

YOUR THOUGHTS:

CHAPTER 20

The Gift of Conviction

6-5-2019

Conviction is a Powerful gift! Conviction means one still has a chance to Yet repent! It's a sign that ones conscious isn't seared with an hot iron, however We shouldn't play around with The Opportunity to Repent.

Read Job 42:6 (KJV)

YOUR THOUGHTS:

CHAPTER 21

Different and Beautiful

6-5-2019

Why would Any One Culture feel as if theirs is better than Another? Obviously, we're All Beautiful to GOD!!! He created us! Everyone can't receive this but for those who can... I Thank GOD for you!!! If you sow hate, you will reap it! Read it!

1 John 4:20

YOUR THOUGHTS:

CHAPTER 22

Retirement

6-6-2019

We mustn't forget that we did Not come to stay!!! Don't Just prepare for retirement Here! Prepare for Eternal Retirement!!! What preparations for the after life are you making? Allowing the worlds view of issues to rule our mindset or decision making isn't wise! We should rather, dig into GODS word and give way to His instructions!

Philippians 3:20&21(KJV)

YOUR THOUGHTS:

CHAPTER 23

It's Not Your Imagination....
You're Discerning

When one has The Holy Ghost, He will show one things The naked eye Can't see! Discernment is So Powerful that It Must be handled With The care of Prayer! This gift isn't given so we can be Judgmental, or to think of ourselves Better than Another; but rather so we can be Wise, Discreet, and Undeceived while helping a brother or sister out when Possible! The thing is, they may Never know your part in their Deliverance and or that you Know what's going on, by your behavior toward he/she, because of the wisdom utilized by you! Read 1 Kings 3:9 (KJV)

YOUR THOUGHTS:

CHAPTER 24

How to Win

It really takes something to Win! One must prepare for it with consistent training to build stamina and not Only that, but one must eat the right foods/fluids and get the necessary amount of rest! Winning looks easy... but there's a Lot that goes into being a Winner! Some win by a technicality! You showed up and they didn't, but yet effort was put into it! Same thing goes for Believers! We must pace ourselves but be consistent! Don't look back because you'll lose ground. Keep moving!

1 Corinthians 9:24 (KJV)

YOUR THOUGHTS:

CHAPTER 25

Make JESUS Famous

Let us make JESUS Famous and Not infamous! Famous is being known for Good or doing Good. Infamous is being well known for doing wrong or negative things! Some may be appalled because Such a statement was made! But look at it this way; when believers behave Unlike CHRIST But state that he/she is a Christian..... it gives the world the Wrong impression/ information about Our LORD! The Gospel is Simple but Powerful Truth, but if we are living in sin but proclaim we are saved.... we bring reproach upon Christ and His Church! This is Very dangerous! The remedy however, is to simply be honest and sincere and live holy by The Power of GOD! He promises to help us do that!

A good scripture is Matthew 5:16 ((KJV)

YOUR THOUGHTS:

CHAPTER 26

History Can Be Amazing

As Amazing as History can be (family, state, national, world etc.) we must use it for good and to propel one forward, and guard our hearts from anger that the knowledge of the past can provoke! You can't help what happened before your existence, good or bad! It is what it is! How ever you and I have entered into this world is out of our hands. This is going to get touchy so prepare your heart! Some are here due to incest, some by rape (those two could be combined), some by choice and others Not! Regardless to How we became beings.... we are, so pull it Together and Live Your Life! Let our Creator heal the deep and painful hurt so you Can move forward by Faith! Let Your history become a Stepping stone into your Dynamic Future instead of a stumbling block!! You choose! A good read is Romans 8:37! (KJV)

YOUR THOUGHTS:

CHAPTER 27

Wait For It.....

"Therefore judge nothing before the time, until the Lord come, who both will bring to light the hidden things of darkness, and will make manifest the counsels of the hearts: and then shall every man have praise of God."

1 Corinthians 4:5 (KJV)

It's Too easy to judge things and matters with what little information we may have, but 1 Corinthians 4:5 plainly tells us to Wait on it! (Paraphrased) On judging of course!!! Flesh is oh too willing to judge people, matters, situations etc., without All the facts. GOD is The Righteous Judge All day and night, but we, on the other hand, must Wait on GODS timing to come to a conclusion of a matter! Get the facts First and Then come to a right conclusion!!! I know what scripture says, further, concerning judging!

"Do ye not know that the saints shall judge the world? and if the world shall be judged by you, are ye unworthy to judge the smallest matters?"

1 Corinthians 6:2 (KJV)

So Yes..., The saints shall judge the world and even the least esteemed Believer should be Able (emphasis on Able- spiritually capable) to judge small matters in the church amongst and between fellow Believers..... but get the facts (truth) first!

YOUR THOUGHTS:

CHAPTER 28

Whose Side Are You Leaning On?

I remember the story in Genesis when GOD through his servant Moses delivered Israel out of Egypt! He did it Mightily!!! They were in bondage 400 years or so, and prayed for deliverance and when it came, they almost didn't recognize it! Many miracles and signs were performed in the process, and they were Finally free from pharaohs chains! While in the desert, they provoked GOD by not trusting Him, although He had Already performed all kinds of miracles for the sole purpose of their freedom! While Moses, afterward, had gone upon Mt. Sinai to speak with The LORD, the people's hearts were leaving GOD Already! When Moses had come down off the mountain, the large group was divided! The question was then proposed, Exodus 32:26 (KJV)

Then Moses stood in the gate of the camp, and said, Who is on the LORD'S side? let him come unto me. And all the sons of Levi gathered themselves together unto him.

You know what happened next, if you know the story (if not please read it)! I understand that it may appear that GOD is taking a long time with the answer to your prayer/s, but Hold on because He is faithful who promised!!! Hebrews 10:23(KJV) (paraphrased). Moses stayed on that mountain 40 whole days! That within itself is Amazing! He aged in GODS' presence! There's so much in that! However, when he came down, he had to get a church out of a church, I like to say right here because some had chosen to worship idols and therefore were destroyed right there! The earth swallowed them up! So allow me to ask the question once again....whose side are you leaning on?! Choose wisely!

YOUR THOUGHTS:

CHAPTER 29

Words and Emotions

There are certain words that, when we hear or read them, stir our emotions. We are living in an emotional, opinionated and offensive time in the earth, not to mention that we are emotional creatures! Of course nothing catches GOD by surprise, and for that reason…, when we are caught by surprise we should turn to GOD immediately, to prevent unnecessary pain!

A good read 1 Corinthians 10:13

YOUR THOUGHTS:

CHAPTER 30

The Ugly Truth!

The truth is always Beautiful, however, the truth can show oneself until he/she doesn't want to see or hear about it! "And ye shall know the truth, and the truth shall make you free". John 8:32 I don't like the stuff about me that isn't godly/holy, however, if it's there… it's there and needs to be dealt with! Adhering to the truth will keep me/you out of Hell! Yes it can hurt, but it's Love! It may Feel ugly, however, Believers know The Truth!

YOUR THOUGHTS:

Printed in the United States
by Baker & Taylor Publisher Services